Comes the Storm

Comes the Storm

Deborah L. Kelly

ISBN: 978-1-989940-66-2
Dimensionfold Publishing
Dimensionfold.com

Acknowledgements

With deep gratitude and respect, I wish to acknowledge I live on the unceded lands of the Nak'azdli Whut'en Nation.

Always first, I would like to thank Father God, for the words (poured into my heart and soul), needed to create this book. All glory goes to the Father; in the holy and sacred name of Christ.

A huge thank you and blessings to Candice James, Poet Laureate Emerita, New Westminster, British Columbia, for her words which adorn the back cover; I am honoured.

I also wish to thank Wendy Van Camp, Poet Laureate, Anaheim, California, for kindly agreeing to do a short review for the back cover of this book. Thank you, Wendy. Blessings.

Thank you to Barbara M. Delong for your words of inspiration on the back of *Comes the Storm.* I wish you every success and many blessings with your new book. I was honored to say a few words on your beautiful poetry and wisdom.

I would like to thank Ken Goudsward, Dimensionfold Publishing in Prince George, British Columbia for the publication of this important book, and for the kindness and support offered during the process. Blessings to you, Ken, for making this happen!

I would also like to thank my wonderful poet sisters, Lozan Yamolky, Janet Kvammen and Sherry Duggal. All of whom are fine poets themselves; thank you ladies for your continued friendship and support in all things creative.

Last, but most certainly not least, all of my friends and fans everywhere; without you, this book would not be possible.

Amen.

*"Choose you this day whom ye shall serve ...
... as for me and my house, we shall
serve the Lord."*

Joshua 24:15

Table Of Contents

Comes the Storm

Comes the storm of prophecy;
a storm humanity could
not envision, even in their
worst nightmares.

It is the storm created by
the warring of light souls
and darkness; they clash
as sparks fly through the four
corners of heaven unto earth.

It is a battle for the salvation
of light and cessation of darkness,
for eternity ~ the final war.

The coming storm is simply a season;
it too shall pass and the light will shine upon
the new earth of the Father's promise.

All Will Be Well

The movement of your hand,
Father God, fills this heart
with awe and wonder; with
each movement your great
Revelation begins now
to manifest its end days
so your children may
understand the works
of your great judgment
and universal truth.

> *Eyes to see, ears to hear;*
> *to know you are near and all*
> *will be well.*

¹In God

I grow in God.
He lights and guides my way
through the storms of this world.

       I live in God.
       He fills my home with the blessing of His
       peaceful and comforting presence.

       I walk with God.
       Each day the Lord takes my right hand;
       He walks with me so that I may never feel alone.

I talk to God.
Each night in my prayers, I ask His forgiveness.
I speak of gratitude and ask mercy for *all of His children.*

       I rest in God.
       I call upon Him to help me with my burdens,
       so I may rest in the warmth of His healing light.

I believe in God.
I feel His presence around and within.
He is the master and helmsman of this ship
in which I travel.

---

¹*Published in the Taj Mahal Review, India 2004*

A Tear Fell

I saw a tear fall to the earth,
it fell from the eye of God.
His sorrow deep, His grief overwhelms with
the loss of so many of His beautiful children.

> *"Choice," He said, "You have a choice*
> *to travel as you wish."*

Yes, He understood the mortal
life of a man when free will was granted.
It is a pity we listen no more.
It is a shame that so many of us have
closed the door to His light.

> Hearts are heavy, life so hard.

> *He cries, "It was never meant to be so.*
> *I have given you gifts, so many*
> *beautiful gifts; you ignore and choose*
> *greed to guide your way.*
> *You choose to wallow in the darkness*
> *offered to you by my once beloved,*
> *greatly illuminated fallen angel, Lucifer ~*
> *his arrogance will leave you undone!*

> Why is it this darkness thrills you so?
> Your rejection of my joy and beauty
> aches within this heart; rain showers
> upon this earth have I given
> to try to heal the damage done.
> All other beings hear my grief
> and sense the tragedy man
> shapes within this world."

Within this vast and living universe
all was considered in His plan
for eternal harmony.
As we give, so must we receive:
law of karma; rhythm of balance.

Too many appeased by the
promise of earthly riches;
sold out to the dark vestiges of power,
and a lust so deep ~ it cannot be erased!

*"I will weep no more for those who are lost,
for judgment day is at hand.
The time quickly approaches; all
will be granted one more chance to return
to my light ~ before I close this door;
create permanent darkness, endless night,
devoid of laughter ~ spiritual blight."*

Hollow Sea

Darkness is not in the business
of fulfilling promises made nor
granting unsustainable wishes;
he deals only in lies and illusion.

> *You will gain none of the riches*
> *you are promised; for now, you*
> *are simply rubbish to eventually*
> *be gotten rid of ~ you are completely*
> *disposable.*

You fell into the illusion and in time
found it had no more substance than
a hologram dragging you down into
a sea of dark mists created only to blind you.

Light Of Grace

As I travel through this raging sea;
this pit, this world of iniquity
I carry your light Lord.
I come ever closer to the safety
of your all-encompassing,
never ending mercy.

> I see around me the bitterness
> which tries to destroy the joy; the bliss
> that you have placed within my heart.
> Your candle burns strong and illuminates
> the darkness as it tries to envelop me.

> *As I travel through this place*
> *protected by your Holy Grace,*
> *a prayer is always in my heart,*
> *of gratefulness that I impart*
> *to you, my God, my shining sea;*
> *my home on your shore of eternity.*

Shining Soul Soldier

As I sit alone I look within myself,
all the anger once here has died.
I find myself looking up at the light
and the blueness of this inner sky.

A realm of peace within my soul;
it has endured for a million years.
The pain: suffering, torment, the woe,
are released with the salt of my tears.

I see the Love held within my heart
God placed it to make me whole;
to bring to earth and spread throughout,
from soul to shining soul.

*Please hear me Lord through my ode to you
as I repent of my earthly sins;
I open my heart to life and to you
so all of your love will shine in.*

Child Of Destiny

Through my eyes as God's witness,
all is illuminated.

The Truth of His Love abounds in my heart.

Praise God ~ Hallelujah, I now see!

*To stand tall in righteousness is to glorify His
name.*

My Faith I store in my heart as I walk through
this place enveloped
and protected
by His Holy Grace.

He has sent us out to the far corners of this earth;
we spread His Word and help others in need
showing them their heavenly worth.

I am the child of a King ~ this I know!

Raise your hearts all His children;
do not compromise your Faith
ever, for this world.

We stand tall, a nation unto the Lord.
I will not break, but will sway gently
with the winds of time; a reed
in a marsh dancing to the music
of this, His great and glorious universe.

[2]Sacred Presence

With Christ in my heart and the peace I see,
I know in my soul, God watches over me
through the hardship and tears; life and its
fears will ne'er sway me.

He holds my hand guiding me toward
the wisdom and understanding of the Divine.
My heart, tried by fire; my soul, awash in an
ocean of tears.

He has taught me through life
there's no reason to fear.

He whispers to me:

> *"My child, be still, I've chosen you*
> *to join others to carry out my will."*

---

[2] *This was written when I was about 21 years old. I knew, even then, we would come to where we are today. I now co-write poetry and have joined with poets around the world; our focus is world peace.*

³Thank You, Lord

Thank you, Lord, for blessings sent;
all the trials you've helped me circumvent.
For tribulations I will never know, which
you will thwart far from my home.
For Love and peace; friends you've lent;
truly, they've been heaven sent.

> Thank you, Lord, for my humble home,
> for all the evils I'll never know.
> Thank you, God, for your kindness too.
> One truly has a friend in you.

---

³ *Published in The Scroll online Christian Newsletter, Special Edition, 2004*

Judas Touch

Shame plays across the faces
of those who have been bought;
a Judas touch in a modern society.

> Cowed by tyranny; in their fear,
> they feel not an inkling of anything
> wrong.

Blinded by the *money*, convinced
the lies and illusions are real ~
they run from the truth while
blaming everyone else for their
weakness.

Emboldened by their penchance
for betraying their fellow mortal,
humans walk forward to their
destiny ~ treason abounds from
country to country.

> Suffering gets worse as the medical
> system is allowed to slowly fall
> apart:
>
> > … discrimination
> > … crime
> > … pedophilia
> > … cannibalism
> > … egoism
> > … debauchery
> > … lust
> > … insanity

… seem to be the mental states in
which
madmen prefer to live.

Mad with power; broken beyond repair,
they take the world hostage ~ their
revenge on a God who no longer
hears them.

Will He show His chosen people
Grace and forgiveness for their
betrayal of His Love; or will
they finally bow down and realize
the power and compassion of
the Omega?

Holy Trinity

I need you to know, when you leave us
God's glorious heaven and His Love await you.
You do not need forgiveness; Christ died that
you would have the Grace of forgiveness:
then, now and always.

It was the promise God made
with His Son's blood.

With Christ's life, death and resurrection
your sins have been covered forevermore
from the Father's sight.

We can only look to Christ with gratitude
for His gift to us of eternal forgiveness.
He paid in full for *our* debt of sin.

You need not leave in sorrow, nor in fear,
only light and peace await you.
You can leave with the Faith and trust
which comes from knowing, you
also are a child of God ~ He is your
true Father.

All He asks is that we believe in His Son,
and what He suffered for you, for me,
and for every one of His children.

If you only believe, He will send His Holy Spirit
of peace and Truth to dwell within you;
He will shine His sacred light through the
darkness.

"I Am the Way, the Truth and the Life."
(John 14:6)

Darkness To Dawn

I can see so clearly, Lord,
your influence in my life.
You're my ship in times of turbulence,
you're my beacon in the night.

You're my compass in the wilderness,
the blizzards of this world.
Without you, Lord, there's nothing:
no light, no warmth, nor pearls.

No riches in the heart of a man
who is Godless in his soul.
No peace, no Love, nor joyfulness;
a human less than whole.

For if a man chooses not to see
the beauty his mortal eyes look upon,
then how does this man ever find his way
from the darkness to the dawn?

Bring God to heart, accept His peace;
His glorious promise of eternity.
In the light of His Grace, let Him shine upon you
as you travel your river to His sea.

In the light and the warmth of His heaven,
He will heal you and shower you with Love.
Let Him shine, let Him glow, let Him into your world;
shining 'pon your life from above.

The Devil's Illusion

Whenever I'm in doubt Lord
or confused about what is near,
I bow my head in prayer and ask
that you please illuminate, make clear
the situation at hand.

I'm never disappointed Lord,
for my prayer is answered the next day.
I thank you, God, for enlightening me
and showing me the way.

> I almost lost my direction, Lord,
> when the devil came to my home.
> He is a master of illusion; almost
> fooled me; I felt so alone.

It was then that I felt a nudge from you
to bow down my head in prayer.
I will never be tempted again, Lord,
without first remembering you're there.

I know that you never turn from me,
though at times, I turn from you;
I also know, I am in your hand
in everything I do.

> *The next time I am tempted*
> *to stray along the way,*
> *I will search my soul for the nudge you give;*
> *get down on my knees to pray.*

⁴They Shall Be Comforted

Hallelujah! Hallelujah!
We, His children, shall weep no more,
for the day quickly approaches
when Christ Himself will even the score.

He'll place His foot upon the earth,
His light will obliterate this world's evil hordes.
Then peace will reign within our hearts
for now until evermore.

> *His Love will pour out freely*
> *upon all His children within the land.*
> *He will show to us His mercy and Grace from*
> *the warmth of His outstretched hand.*

He'll stroke the sorrow from our brows;
forgiveness will shine through
from the giving touch of His heart to ours ~
all His children shall live in His Truth.

> Until the day when He arrives,
> He's placed His trust in those whom He loves.
> His Grace will shine on all the land
> from His Kingdom on high, see the sun in the sky;
> this world will bask in the warmth of His glory,
> and mourning shall be nevermore.

---

⁴ *Written with empathy for the loss of so many of my American brothers and sisters who died on September 11, 2001.*

Rest

Early morning has blossomed;
night's rest sustains my soul
through daylight hours.

> *I wish I could capture in a photo,*
> *the view from my eyes with all*
> *the richness and depth.*

So many varying shades of green
blending beautifully across the land.
Trees stand tall in reverence, arms
lifted to the magic of heaven.

Grandmother moon shines her
beauteous illumination across
the land.

> Behind the clouds, grey or white,
> the Lord sits peering out upon
> the children of man …

> … so lost, so lost in the web of life.

> *So lost my children ~ follow me;*
> *I shall give you rest.*

[5]To Sing With His Angels

As I drifted off to sleep
God's angels came to me;
lifted me up in the arms of Love
with their chorus of liberty.

I sang among God's angelic choir,
I was blessed by the Host of Hosts;
I felt within the joy, the peace
of Christ's blessèd and Holy Ghost.

I sang with rapturous splendour;
felt the miracle within my soul.
This is how it was meant to be:
complete, serene and whole.

Come raise your voices to the sky
God's children join in harmony;
sing from the depths of your graceful soul,
blessèd Lord, you have come to save me.

I'll sing His praises to the world
in my mortal, earthly form.
I'll walk through this world in His merciful embrace,
with His help, I can weather all storms.

---

[5] *This poem was written from an experience I had while I slept. You and I both know it was **not** just a dream.*

So raise your hearts up to the sky;
in the clouds with His glory He comes.
The rapture will lift us to His kingdom of light.

His heart will shine through, His Love will be true;
we'll be blessed with the gift of new sight.

⁶Yh Wh

I look out upon a land
made of crystal and lace;
Lady Hoar makes her
appearance known.

> *Dazzled by her great*
> *beauty; her wondrous love*
> *of the earth is on display;*
> *this great Love, Divine*
> *in its source.*

Silent world: fresh air,
clean well water, and fertile
land to grow and prosper.

Gratitude flows from
my pores as I breathe;
with each breath, a
whisper of His name.

Yh …
Wh …

Peace be with you
in the Spirit of the Lord.

---

⁶ *As you breathe in ... Yh. As you breathe out ... Wh In essence, we*
speak the Father's name with each breath we take.

Oasis

In the midst of this barren desert;
the acrid streets of society,
I have found an oasis
whose waters flow into you.

> You shall awaken your people
> and show them the path to salvation.

A human heart, a loving heart
shall be given; a path paved with
mercy and Grace; a world
of rainbows in your space.

> *Your commandments engraved*
> *on the soft hearts of your children.*

A garden of delights;
senses blend, and all vibrance
collected of your universe is
spent from the bounty of the soul.

> *Tried of sorrow; honed in pain,*
> *with everything, the salt of things ~*
> *we've everything to gain.*

From long-suffering hardships
to the cruelest this plane can give;
even with all its harshness, it is priceless,
this life which we live.

My Will Unto His Will

I truly am a happy soul
as I travel through this world;
I look for all the wondrous things.

> *God's magic surrounds me.*
> *I watch it all awaken before my eyes.*

I look not upon this life
through the eyes of the human;
but, through the veil of His light:
His Truth, and this gentle,
compassionate heart which
He has placed within me.

With this Love, this light and this laughter
He brings, I feel the joy of each little moment.
I take the time to notice another's heart,
be it kind or be it dark.

> *I will give to others whatever*
> *His will commands I share.*

His blessings abound, and I feel
the miracle of creation all around
and throughout this life I live.

> *It is my will unto His will.*
> *I give freely and with joy.*

It is His will guiding this heart:
it is His Love caring for my world;
most importantly, it is His heaven
I have been blessed with
as I journey this mortal place.

> In His care, with His protection,
> He bids me, *"Walk within my Grace."*

Lost

The Lord's original plan;
that we all live peacefully,
in harmony with one another
to learn the lessons of this
wide and beautiful universe.

    Somehow, we have become lost,
    as sheep who find themselves in a pasture
    of desolate waste and despair.

    We have lost our way and have fallen
    into a world of darkness and greed;
    all consuming passions of selfishness
    and inconsiderate attitudes toward
    our fellow man.

    Flesh of one flesh;
    of the same blood we flow.

    Humankind was shaped and molded
    from the purity of goodness and of God's
    selfless thought so He be not alone.

Instrument Of Light

A fine tuned instrument
honed from the stores of His own heart;
engraved and molded from the precious
metals of the soul: courage, strength;
yes, weakness too.

⁷*He then etches His signature upon each.*

We all belong to the light.
Transparent in mortal sight;
of substance seen through
the eyes of inner being.

Enlightenment: a place of solitude,
of oneness, sometimes aloneness;
individual through all this great universe.

We must learn to hear, have our
ear ever upon the whisper within us.
An angel's caring, soothing voice;
guiding hand.

*Reach up, touch the sky with everything you are,
and all you hope to be.*

---

[7] *In recent DNA studies, they have determined the mathematics of two strand DNA adds up to 144,000 (God's signature); He will arrive with 144,000 Saints. They also discovered in the recent changes (man-made), to DNA with the addition of a strand to make it three strand, the mathematics add up to 216,000 (the signature of darkness). This latter number was achieved by multiplying 600x60x6 (number of the beast: six hundred three score and six).*

Witness To A Miracle

The Love and admiration of a young child;
is this not the greatest gift God has to offer?
The concept of life, love, children,
man and woman molded from clay
and cast in blood, sinew and bone,
is sacred in His sight.

> To be created with such a deep capacity
> for love and compassion; truly, this shows
> the beauty and miracle of God in His
> infinite wonder.

We have been tried in our Faith.
We have created our own nightmares,
sorrows, tears; though we have suffered,
Faith has grown a thousand-fold;
life has become ever so precious.
I was afraid in the beginning;
afraid to let go of the rational and put
my child's life in the Lord's hands.

> I was so afraid at that time He would not
> give her back to me.

Then, I saw His promise reflected upon her face.
The bright light of God's healing reached
out and touched my soul.
A promise made to a silent and suffering heart.

I will continue to walk with the Lord
through my life.

*I will look to His wisdom when hardship
visits my home; I will remember His
comfort and the power of His Love
at work in my life; most importantly, I will say,
"Thank you, God," every day of my life,
"for giving my child the blessing
of your miracles."*

In The Light Of God

I pray dear Lord, please come and see
the darkness and shadows; they try
to devour me.

> I stand for light I live in Truth;
> do they not know I'm protected by you?
> Come clear my sight, chase these shadows away,
> lead me back to your garden in which your children
> now play.

Come take my hand, lead me through
the maze of evil which challenges you.
Show them Lord, how you watch over your fold;
let them know that it is your hand I hold.

Bring back the peace they have tried to steal;
shine your light so that I may clearly see
the path to your salvation; to your Love, your mercy;
to your Grace.

Let them know they can never tarnish this soul.

This spirit is a part of all that is you.
My heart's been made soft and filled with your Truth.
You have opened a door so that I may walk through
leaving shadows behind, I walk beside you.

Just when the darkness seems too hard to bear,
I look into the light and you show me you're there.

Chilled Beauty of Morning

Each day, I look out my window
upon this land, and my eyes,
served a feast of beauty, are
awed by His Grace and magic.

>The quiet whisper of night's
>silence on a country street;
>deer peer around the corner
>with curiosity in their dark,
>beautiful eyes.

The chilled beauty of morning;
Jack's sister has passed through
the night hours; lace and crystal
shine and twinkle with the early sun.

>*Crisp beauty surrounds the now:*
>*cool, clean, fresh air fills my body*
>*to overflowing. A prayer of thanks*
>*for this world of peace my eyes*
>*are blessed to look upon.*

When I look up to this sacred and holy sky above me,
I know, without doubt, His covenant with His children;
a promise made, will be honoured;
His Truth shall set us free.

Shadows

I stand strong in His word,
I've done nothing wrong;
it is not my concern
you can't hear my song.

I try hard in life
to be a happy soul;
this world begrudges
one who has found peace within.

It has not been an easy journey,
and it has at times, obscured
the sun as it tries to shine
into my heart and my life.

        I will not allow another who is
        obsessed with selfish concerns
        to pull me down from my sky.
        I will not sell out to you;
        not obliged to say why!

I will not compromise my values
nor will I play the role of hypocrite.
I will tell you honestly, since you now ask;
there's been too much hurt already in my past.

I stand strong in God's Faith;
I willingly share of my heart
with another who truly does care.

    The clouds have been lifted from before my eyes;
I can once again look up, Lord, and see clearly your blue

skies.

I Cried

An angel came and took
me into heaven.
The world remained on
self-destruct behind me …

… I cried

tears for those I have loved
who could not see heaven as I did;
tears for the beauty that
man had destroyed
through his selfishness …

… I cried

tears for the beautiful child
I had to leave behind
in a world of such sorrow and suffering.
Did the stairs lead to His kingdom …?

… I cried

colours; a reflection of my soul
climbing, climbing; I've stopped …

*… it is here I will rest and play
within the kingdom of God's soul.*

Cleansing

Human hearts connected by
silver thread to the Divine
are soft and reverent in their
view of the world as darkness
grows.

       Insidious tentacles reaching
       out, trying to permeate every
       aspect of life.

       The time given this beast is
       limited by the Father in His
       cleansing of humanity.

For every sin, there shall be
forgiveness given each one
who keeps the sacred and Divine
within their heart.

Lend Me Your Strength, Lord
(A Prayer)

I get down on my knees to you, my Lord;
I pray from the depths of my heart.
I ask you please help me through this trial?
Show me where to begin, where to start
to battle the demons around me;
to know what to say and then when;
to quiet the indignation I'm feeling
when I see the unfairness of sin.

The depths of true injustice;
raging madness of corporeal whims:
unharnessed, undisciplined and spoiled
soul consumed and destroyed from within.

> *The damage of deceit and misdirection:*
> *there is hurt from uncompassionate deeds.*

I witness your Truth all around me;
there are others who are willing to see
the reality of your bright and wondrous radiance,
everywhere and anywhere you may be.

> *If we stand strong and honourable*
> *in the beauty of your Faith ~ we will win!*

As I prepare to go into battle
to defend the honour you give;
I put on your armor of light deep and strong.

> *I shall grow in your Grace, as I fight for my place,*
> *ever remembering your victory song.*

[8]Land To Land

I feel the mourning surrounding me
on this anniversary of 9-11.
I feel the sorrow of my fellow man
as he flounders to rebuild God's sun.
So many heroes died that day
in senselessness and in vain;
the glory of His comfort
shall in our hearts ever remain.

>We tried so hard to understand
>how humanity could be so cruel;
>The vileness of Satan and his evil hordes,
>we pray, will soon become powerless tools.

In the hearts of all survivors
of this heinous act there stands:
Hope, Faith and Love within
that with the dove, fly land to land.
We join our hands in prayer for those
who left us on that day;
we know within our grieving
the Lord will have His say.
Send your prayers up to His world;
give your grief to God above.

>*He will heal this world, He will change our sight*
>*with the gift of His glorious Love.*

---

[8] *This was written in loving memory for all who died on that fateful day, September 11, 2001. They are in our hearts ~ always.*

Do Not Fear

A prayer of gratitude,
Lord, for the blessing
of a new day

> Heart plays a tune within;
> percussion in sync with
> the music of the spheres.

We will dance and sing
with the angels; laughter
and light shall be
the rhythm for our feet.

Shall we meet just inside
Heaven's gate; we cannot
be late for the great
and merciful Father tends
us all with His Love and
forgiveness.

> *Sing your songs of joy*
> *and blessing, for a new world*
> *will soon be here ...*

> ... do not fear.

Beautiful World

I thank you, God, for the beautiful things,
for your love of me and such wonderful wings.
To soar above in heaven's sky; to see an eagle,
or hear a sigh.

For pain and laughter, compassion too;
hope and Faith and the knowledge of you.
I praise you God, as you rest on high
for the colour of a flower, the blueness of the sky …

     … for the trees of the forest, it is here
     wild creatures abound.
     As I walk through your glorious Eden
     there is no absence of sound.

Your voice echoes in the willows,
your presence surrounds this timeworn heart.

I sing hallelujah!

     For love and for pain and the tears mortals cry;
     I praise you for helping me see through clear eyes.
     I thank you for showing me light, and the Truth;
     for the mysteries of age and the wonders of youth.

Thank you, Lord, for the stars in the sky:
for the sound of the rain; a newborn's first cry,
for the wisdom of elders and birds in the trees …

  … for teaching me how to pray when on bended knee to
you; the promise of forever, tomorrow will be brand new.

Crucified

I hang upon a cross beside you, Lord,
the woman and the sin;
I feel the salt of your tears
and the torment you feel within.

How could God's children, other mortals,
your own flesh and blood, be so brutally cold?
Destroying the man, destroying the temple,
though they ne'er came close to your soul.

As my temple dies here beside you, Lord,
you take my hand in your hand, and you say:

> *"For your gift of compassion and repentance,*
> *you shall follow me all the way from this world*
> *to my Father's great kingdom; this shall end*
> *as a great and blessèd, glorious day.*
> *Because you hold Faith in my death*
> *and my spirit's ascension to peace,*
> *I will bless you forever sweet child of mine;*
> *eagle's wings you shall know to fly free.*

Lifted

Thank you, God, for the gifts you bring,
I am lifted up, can you see my heart sing?
Thank you, too, for the prayers you have heard,
you have blessed me Lord, with the gift of your Word.
You have answered my prayers, each one I have said,
you have brought me to hope in a world I thought dead.
You have lifted me up, given me wings now I fly;
I soar ever upward in the light of your sky.

In my heart there lies a rhapsody of colour and of Truth,
you have shown to me true beauty, you have blessed my
view.

You have opened my door to the love and the light;
my heart will never again know the night.
You have scattered the path before me with peace,
You have brought me to healing; I bathe in your sea
of Love and of Grace, forgiveness and Faith,
all I can do while here is just wait.

For I know that your kingdom is so close to hand,
you'll bring harmony and justice to all in this land.
The kingdom of God lies deep in our souls,
it's up to us to find the true road.

I will spread your word to all who will hear;
you will shine on me, you are always near.

You hold my right hand, I am never alone;
at the end of my days, I will gently go
home.

His Presence

In the hearts of the righteous
His light burns deep and strong
illuminating all around;
true hearts can hear His song.

In God's world there is laughter:
love and harmony; the riches of
infinite Wisdom.

In her glory, she walks with me.

I feel the angel's presence when
upon my knees in prayer.
A quiet, touching energy
surrounds me in the air.

I meditate and listen to
the silent voice inside of me;
it's everywhere and anywhere,
resonant and free.

As I Receive

I write those things my
muse brings to me.
I am an old-fashioned poet.

> I care not about today's
> big and fancy words used
> only to impress and feed
> one's ego, when *simple*
> could say it so much better.

I care not about being
politically correct ~ rubbish!

> *I write truth from the heart,*
> *not the mind.*

I write with varying
emotions, which depend
upon those presented
in the ether; even though
seen in the physical
world by my muse.

> *It all comes from His generous*
> *cup of creation.*

I change very few words other
than those which my mortal
ear has a hard time hearing.

> As I receive is as I write.

> *Blessèd be; I am held in His light.*

In Times Of Darkness

I run to my protection
in the fortress of my Lord;
ask of Him His shelter from
this cruel world's evil hordes.
They hammer me on all sides,
try to make me bow in shame;
blaming me with all their lies
as they play their wicked games.
I wear the shining armor of God,
His light surrounds my being.

I live in the Faith He will save
His child from all things deceiving.

I carry strong before me, His shield
of Faith, His divine Grace;
I know with perseverance He will
lead me from this place.
This place where evil lives disguised,
covered in lamb's finest wool;
this place where liars gather thinking
God's children only fools.
I know I am surrounded by
warring angels sent by Him;
Christ will guide me safely through
and protect me from their sin.

They cannot blame nor hurt me,
as long as I hold my Saviour's hand;
for all their crimes and trying,
they'll end up in the devil's land.
They shall be sent to rest with Satan
to deal with their sin and deadly ways,

and will be given to eternal hellfire
in the pit's unholy maze.
Lying is a sin used by those who live
in the darkness of their own soul.
It will tear dark hearts to pieces,
chew them up and eat them whole.

> I know in this world of evil,
> of darkness and of lies
> many dare to doubt His word;
> have no fear of their demise.

> *I say unto those who rush toward*
> *their death as an evil one;*
> *think twice about the path you trod,*
> *it's awfully cold without God's Son.*

You'll find naught but His damnation;
eternal pain, if you choose
to walk without His Son
and it's Satan's hand you hold.
For my God is a jealous God
and will not tolerate your disdain.
He'll cast you from His garden
and won't care how cold your rain.

> *So come, my Lord, see how evil tries*
> *to thwart the plan you have written for this*
> *child of yours, as I rest in Christ's warm hand.*

I will sing your praises, Lord, as I travel through the pain,
knowing that I will come through this season;
I will rest in your peace once again.

Sweet Child Of Mine

Walk with me, sweet child of mine
and in my kingdom you shall play.
You'll stand beside my eternal Son
as His witness to judgment day.
You'll walk the streets of this earthly home
protected by His Holy Ghost.
You'll be given all the things you need
and the gifts you have wanted the most.
I'll shower you with riches
of the soul, sweet honey wine.
I'll show you how the rainbow is made,
surround you with angels as you travel through time.
I'll bless you with the gift of Love,
wisdom shall be placed within your heart.
I'll give to you directly from my stores,
where you'll never, ever see dark.
I'll cover you with forgiveness,
you are mortal and will sometimes fall.
You could never displease me my righteous child,
your Faith in me will help you stand tall.
When your world gets hard to bear
and the sorrow just runs too deep,
I'll hold you up in the palm of my hand
and wipe away the tears that you weep.
I'll replace them with the joy of my Son's blessèd
spirit and unconditional Host;
the hurt inside will be easier to bear,
He'll help you carry your load.

So carry a peaceful countenance, my child
and your cross will be
easier to hold.
I will shine on you, as the
sun will too
wherever in this world you
may go.

Healing Winds

For every darkness suppressed,
for every major sin that goes unresolved
and lies hidden inside,
a tear forms in the fabric of one's soul.
Left untended, and in the dark,
the light is slowly diminished
lest the breeze of healing comes.
Lord, I see so many turning away from
your gift of Love, putting their
Faith into things of no worth;
no value in your world,
they dissolve into earth.

> *A new god arises from within this society;*
> *money: green and greedy,*
> *with a never-ending lust for power.*
> *Society has lost its way; we shame*
> *ourselves with sin and disgraceful actions.*

The Father's eyes shed tears of blood,
placed by the pain of being unable to help
a wanton child; terrified, body defiled
with the torments of abuse and self-blame.
A tear falls inside; into the sea and its tide
of emotions that wax in ones heart.
The sea, with this tear, hears the sorrow,
feels the fear of a heart torn to pieces by time's winds.
Forgiveness through the leaves of the trees
which line this shore, line one's spirit with a
salve to help us heal.

The joy, the blessèd joy we feel
when we come into the son, out of the rain.
There's a rainbow shining through
on the other side of you.
The sun will always shine again,
when you come out in the breeze
beyond the pain.

Do You...?

When you look into my world what is it that you see?
Do you recognize the Truth? It lives inside of me.
Do you see who I Am, can you feel what I feel?
Is this all in my mind or could it be real?
Do you see as I see with the eyes of the soul?
Do you see just a part or do you view as a whole?
Do you elaborate on colour, can you sing with the wind?
Do you know where your love is, can you find it within?
Do you know where your heart lives, do you walk in the
light?
Do you feel warm in His love on a cold winter's night?

> Do you fly with the angels?
> Do you soar o'er the clouds?

Do you sing with His choir, do you praise Him aloud?
Do you walk away from shadows, can you laugh through
the tears?
Do you see only youth or are you burdened by years?
Do you wander along in a desolate sea, to find your road
to eternity?
Do you dare, in this world, risk persecution in His name?

> *I don't hesitate! Part of me is to blame*
> *for the sin, the humiliation, the horrors, the shame;*
> *He bore these in silence and never laid blame.*

A man of the noblest, mightiest light;
a human, a mortal, yet, immortal inside.
A man of humility, blessèd in God's Grace
Christ bore with integrity man's sin and disgrace.

Ghost Raven

Ghost Raven calls through
the forest ~ there is danger in
this land!

> *Haunting, urgent; a warning*
> *to be heard by all, man and beast*
> *alike.*

A storm comes; it rises, comes
closer; an energy, a sense we must
not ignore.

> All creatures of this earth feel
> energy and vibrational change;
> watch and learn.
> > Our sun gets hotter each year:
> > rivers, lakes … go dry,
> > food dies on the branch; withering
> > in the intense heat.

Water becomes harder to find,
for most of it has been poisoned
by our own carelessness.

> Ghost Raven knows the secrets
> of humans; haunting cries
> will not stop until the world
> begins to listen.

> > *Haunting, pleading cries to*
> > *mortals drift upwards through*
> > *the ether; sadly, these cries fall*
> > *upon too many deaf ears.*

The Sword Of God

A two-edged sword honed in honour and Truth.
One edge cuts swiftly with precision to
the marrow of the sinner's bone.
This edge, drips with the blood of sin;
the sinner, forever unable to hide within
from the razor sharp steel of the Lord's judgment.

> The other, laced with the fine sweetness
> of the Lord's light and Grace,
> illuminates the child of God on
> spirit's journey through this place.
> Don't think to challenge nor duel with
> this, His blade of immortal steel;
> what you find in your heart determines
> the edge by which you shall be judged.

A righteous child will find only joy and Love;
the sinner will find darkness,
and the endless abysmal flames
of hatred surrounding him;
he shall never be freed.

> Once this decision is made in the heart
> there is no turning back, the days
> of forgiveness, almost spent; the Lord's
> kindness has been lent for your eternal score.
> To think that one can change decisions
> made in rage; one more chance
> to say, *"I'm sorry, hear me Lord,"*
> will be offered in the end days of this life.

Those who are given the divine beauty
of the spirit body, new and bright,
need never ask to be heard,
for the Lord already knows each word
spoken in the heart; directed
heavenward in earnestness and in Truth.

That you understand the consequence of the
knowledge you have gained; be it good or be it dark.
He will touch you in the place where soul
lives; His light will forever guide your way
as you travel your path home to His cosmos this day.

He told us He is " *... the Way, the Truth and the Life ...* "
John 14:6

Gone Are The Days Of War

Comfort; knowing
love is showing.
Love is healing;
heart is reeling,
peace ~ is coming
in a UFO!
No more fighting;
fast as lightning ~
this world is about to change!
No more illness;
only wellness.
No more war;
nevermore.
No more sorrow;
a better tomorrow.
No more weeping;
our smiles we're keeping.
No more heartbreak;
walk through Heaven's gate.
No more madness;
simply gladness.
No more hatred;
Satan's gated
in the hellfire's of karma.
No more shadow;
only light, glorious light!
No more dying;
no more crying.
The guff is empty;
souls aplenty.

No more guns, and no more bombs;
gone are the days of war.

54

[9]Unto Heaven

Forcing unhealthy masks on
society has nothing to do with
concern for your well-being ~
but everything to do with control
of the masses.

They are *scam masters* who hire
the clowns of Hollywood to act
out their scenarios of destruction.

Why would you *ever* believe world
leaders and corporations have
compassion for your losses?
For there will be many.

*Have you made your peace with
the Divine? You will need Him
desperately in the not too distant
future.*

Raise your voices unto Heaven.

---

[9] *Centre of the Bible: Psalm 118:8 "It is better to trust in the
Lord than to put confidence in man."*

An Angel's Kiss

As I lay here in my bed this night
I feel the whisper of angel's wings.
Their gentle kisses upon my cheek;
nudging me to join them for awhile
as I gently drift off to sleep.

I was lifted up softly in robes of white
with an angel on each side,
guiding and holding me, whispering
soothing words of Faith which
drifted before me in their sky.

*"We teach you to fly; we show you
the path that will always lead you home
when you need to renew, and heal
the sorrow within.
We show you a place of peace,
a refuge for your heart.
The Father has sent us, to lift you up.
[10]He has granted you the Grace of His wonder,
and the spirit joy of His heaven."*

To behold such glory, to feel with such tenderness;
to breathe in with such awe; I cannot tell you
what I saw as I journeyed; there are no mortal
expressions to convey what it was
I experienced this day.

An Angel's kiss God sent my way.

---

[10] *Ephesians 2:8-9 "For by grace are ye saved through faith; and that not of yourselves, it is the gift of God: Not of works, lest any man shall boast."*

His Eden Returns

Our leaders rush toward death and decay
     with the obsession for war in their hearts.
     Do they even stop for a moment?
     Do they even hear what the people say?

> *Their evil can't wait; their power puffed up,*
> *they rush toward judgment day.*

Do they realize the consequences of their actions?
     Do they know where the prophecy leads?
     Do they have any idea it's their death in the end;
     they think they'll be the victors, hence, their
     horrible lies they will always defend?

Fools, desperate fools, hiding behind the masks
they display to try to keep the peace within
their own quaking souls; somewhere inside,
they know they can't hide from the Truth.

     His time is near to hand; many are not watching.
       No attention do they pay to the signs
all around us; followers are led to the day their
leaders have promised will end all the fear
in their hearts, but they have no intention
of telling the people; they forgot to mention
it is only their greed and self-proclaimed glory
they wish to feed.

The death of innocent people means nothing
to those who distort and disfigure God's Truth.
They will pay with their souls; forget they have gold,
it will mean nothing when Christ takes His stand.

*The gentle and strong among His children will inherit
this glorious land; Eden, once again, will stand strong.*

Of His Love

I hear the sigh of angels
as they circle 'round this night;
sheltering me from darkness
bringing with them heaven's light.

       I feel the breath of angels
       as they protect me through the years.
       They surround me with a halo of mercy;
       breathe comfort while I cry my tears.

       I can see this circle of angels,
       I can feel myself standing in their radiant light.
       As long as they stand and walk with me
       I shall never again know the night.

I can hear the chorus they're singing
bringing joy in their harmony above,
and God, in His infinite wisdom
reveals, the glorious song of His Love.

Witness

As I look up into the night sky
I see the velvet silhouetted reflection
of this great and vast universe.
I feel the eye of Truth that
follows where I travel,
to unravel the great mystery
of this beautiful blessing;
this *life* granted me
from the power and glory
of His wish that I should exist.

I, as all others in this beautiful Eden,
He breathed into existence; now
granted Grace, at His urgence
I should walk in His peace.
I am free in my heart,
no prejudice do I impart
to my fellow man.

It is His design I stand
as witness to the pride;
the arrogance of man.
My brethren surround me
in the magnitude of this,
the great plan of creation.

I move to the sound of the heavenly spheres,
my elation grows wings, my heart
in rhapsody sings the great song
of His heavenly choir
until the sound of His voice
lifts me higher and higher.

[11]Without You, Lord

Without your sacrifice, Lord,
there would be no life eternal,
it would all be an inferno of sin
and darkest despair.

> Without your blood, Lord,
> there would be no promise
> of your hereafter; there would
> be no laughter, no joy to unfold;
> your story never heard ~ never told.

> > Without your forgiveness, Lord,
> > it would be a barren wasteland
> > of human lusts and desires;
> > a funeral pyre for the souls
> > of the innocent.

Without your light, Lord,
the path to eternity would be
dark and treacherous; full of holes,
placed there to trip the souls of
those unfortunate enough
to have lost their way.
They've given up at the end of the day.

> > > *Without your Grace, Lord,*
> > > *and a hold on your Faith,*
> > > *what a terrifying place this would be.*

---

[11] *This poem was inspired by the movie, The Passion of the Christ. I wept.*

Without your love for us, Lord,
there would be no ability to be one
with all which surrounds and envelops us
within this, your great and magnificent Eden.

The rose would never bloom,
there would never be a tune of
the spheres around us.
So let us share a prayer of gratitude
for the latitude He allows us
in His ability to forgive our sinful ways.

*Let us hope for laughter, for the
joy of ever-after; let us sing
the wondrous song of Christ in praise.*

The Pale Steed

Crime increases; darkness spreads.
People are dying; too many now dead.
Hell has come to earth on the heels
of the pale steed named Death …

    … his breath is foul.

    He breathes in fear, breathes out death.

    It is up to each which they let in ~ light
    or darkness?

Remember, fear is a tool of the dark;
beware what you choose to see and feel!

Let us hearken unto Christ and His
angels; let us praise God in his judgment,
for it is good; it is just.

    "Vengeance is mine," saith the Lord.

    In the beginning, there was … the Word.

¹²I Remember The Children

I remember the children the most, Lord;
the ones you called back home
when they were so ill.
You could not heal them here,
their lessons were learned.
Back to your resplendent kingdom;
returned home to bathe
in the healing light of your great
and glorious Love.

I remember the children the most, Lord;
their smiles lit up lives, their
hearts were soft and as sad as ours
as we all travelled the same road,
hoping and praying, along with
all the other parents, for our children;
all hoping you could somehow
lighten their load ~ it is far too heavy
for a little child to hold.

I remember the children the most, Lord;
my sorrow meant so little
in comparison to the
crosses they carried.
Some were heavier than others,
some light, but all were so
very hard to hold.

---

¹² *This poem was inspired in 1991, while I sat on the cancer ward at BCCH, tending to my daughter as she fought cancer. I was so saddened by the children suffering around me. My daughter did survive, and we are now 30+ years and two grandchildren later.*

This illness they had tried
to drown each soul in the darkness
of forever, where disease
has a normal name;
a major player in evil's game.

But the light of the Lord lives ever in the hearts
of His dear children, no matter the age
on the mortal plane: we are all His children,
we are all loved the same.

¹³He Spoke To Me

I burst into being, a spirit of great light,
it was definitely God's voice I heard on that night.
In the midst of my shadows when the fear was so strong
He made a path to my heart to soothe me in song.

The song of His voice as it surrounded mortal sin;
still, with forgiveness, He invited me in
to the isle of Paradise where all is serene,
and brought me His comfort through a terrifying dream.

His voice it surrounded me, felt within and without.
A voice that I knew, there's no inkling of doubt.
It was everywhere and nowhere, heard above and below;
it rippled through bone, through the heart of this soul.

It bolted into my world from a sky filled with Love,
flew into my soul as God's peaceful dove.
I could feel as it touched every chord in this heart;
as light filtered through me and took away shadow's dark.

---

[13] *Again, another dream which was, truly, not just a dream ~ I swear the night I dreamt this, I was having the most terrifying nightmare I have ever experienced. Since this experience (some 25-30 years ago), I have not had another nightmare. As I witnessed His great Light and Power, it filled me with awe.*

It was loud, it was soft, it was vibrant and calm,
the voice of acceptance, protection and awe.
I heard it all around me and just knew it was He;
I could tell by the beauty He washed over me.

*I have never again seen such wonder in dreams
and sometimes I wonder, did I actually hear Him?
Did I, in Truth, hear God as I slept trembling in
nightmare's way,
or was it just an uttered prayer ~ something I needed on
that day?*

I Just Asked

I thank you so much, Lord,
for helping me win the war.
For showing my enemies that
I am worthy of your Grace.
I just asked.

You brought me peace.

I am so filled with gratitude, Lord;
you always bring me back when
I have lost my way.
You have taken the shadows
out of my day.
I just asked.

You brought me light.

I will sing praises, Lord,
for your mercy and your
Love in my life;
for the path you illuminate
to see me safely through the strife.
I just asked.

You brought me hope.

I will remain humble upon this journey, Lord,
for you have shown me the
path to light, hope, and peace.
You have blessed me with
forgiveness and the light
that is truly me.
I just asked; *You taught me to see.*

Unholy Soul

The unkindness, selfishness around me;
it tires me, and I wonder what reward would
one hope to obtain by being mean-spirited
and inconsiderate?
Small minded people; little souls
that have sold out in the hopes
they will receive some of the spoil.
Without toil or patience, shadow souls
hope to drink from the cup
of a rich man's scraps.
No conscience breaks through a
wall that's consumed with defense;
no matter what the cost to the soul already lost
in the greed and cowardice of untruth.

Pretense saturates an unholy heart.

Someone who died before they ever started to live;
couldn't give, couldn't exist without the deceitful
dreams unkindness and profit bring.
To do these things, no matter the requirement,
to sacrifice an innocent soul, how can another
not see the hole carved out in the darkness
of their own heart?

From the path of salvation an unholy
soul departs.

Minion

My prayers go out to all
those women/men who had/have
no idea of the minion
in the person they chose to love.

A marriage surely made in hell.

... Minion.

I envision one in particular
who seemed to be
a good and loving mother
and kind soul ... a woman who
truly loves her man.

... Minion.

Not much is seen or heard of/from
her in recent times ~ though from
what I have gleaned, she has been
smeared.

... Minion.

I sense, certainly, she now lives
every woman's worst nightmare.

... Minion.

Crumbled Wings

In the middle of ground zero
the Lord's cross marks the tragedy
of the day of shadows, visited
upon so many; empty violence,
senseless calamity ~ Satan's pride.
Let us never forget the colour
of Satan's dark hand as he
spreads his violence throughout
the land of dreams; give him
no room to tear the seams of
society's heart ~ depart evil
one, move over, return to
your darkness, for the sun
of God's light shall burn what
is left of your crumbled wings!
They carry you no more.
Vengeance has singed the flesh from
wings that once flowed with the
luminosity of heaven.
Now, as those wings drip
the darkness from whence you have
come ~ go back to hell darkened one,
deliver a message to the minions you lead …
God still lives; Truth still
gives heart peace.

Your vain attempts at retribution
rebound and send you further into the pit.
You can climb no higher from
your raging sea of flames;
as God's new order arrives
and takes its place upon His beautiful,
green planet earth.

The name of darkness
shall be forgotten as the Father's
children look out upon His shining
sea of forgiveness, coming to know,
no matter how dark
the dark, nor how boundless the
sea of Satan's calamity, the light of heaven
will always shine on the children of God
and salvation shall be our glorious reward!

Darkness Came To My Door

Darkness came to my door one night
'neath the cover of December moon;
found it was not my time to leave,
he had come for me too soon.

> I don't know why he would waste his time
> coming for someone he cannot see;
> he knows, without doubt,
> it's the Lord's hand I hold;
> he'll never, ever be able to take me.

Darkness stood and looked as if
he had been fooled by God one more time.
Shadow should know he's not welcome here,
I don't know why he keeps trying.

> *I stood and I laughed as darkness went pale*
> *when he saw the flash of the Lord's power*
> *this night.*
> *Darkness swore he'd never come near me again*
> *'cause he couldn't deal with such a radiant light.*

Sorrow Owned
(A Prayer)

Every day in my heart
you are surrounded by angels,
and a prayer; this prayer,
sent upon the wings of
Love's essence upward
to heaven, through the mist
of wishes and dreams come true.

      I walk with you, even though you
      appear to walk alone.
      I wish you humility, so
      you may shine with the radiance
      of a new found light.
      I wish you Faith so you
      may traverse the crevices of
      evil's quake, as you walk upon
      the unseen Eden that surrounds you.
      I wish you peace, so you
      may know that those who walk
      within Love's hand; walk hand in hand
      through the hardship of the heart.
      It concerns us one and all, for
      every fall, there is a scar;
      a tear of sorrow owned.
      Another piece of the sadness
      is now healed; the real,
      the Truth, the beauty of
      Love's good heart revealed.

There Is A Soul

There is a soul who lives within
a crystal palace dream.
He watches, sees with spirit eyes,
everything we do; everywhere we've been.
A spirit of tremendous Love
looks upon me at every moment.
        What is it, I wonder, which
        makes me so significant in the eyes
        of such a dazzling and omnipotent being?

To think, He sees what I'm seeing;
He knows my next step, yet wonders
if I will succeed in staying on my feet.
Will this challenge bend the
bow of my heart to the point of breaking
or, will it end up making me stronger,
filling my heart with His Faith
and His beautiful, vibrant rainbows?
I must await His time. I must
learn patience and peace; be still.
Beauty venerated; hear these words
little child of mine:

"All that I own in this
vast universe, my home;
I give to you here, so you don't
feel alone.

It won't be so easy, there will
be challenges along the way.
But once you reach Love's summit ~
you will see, it's a radiant day!"

Add Unto Me

As you pour the answer to my prayer
       into the well deep inside my heart, Father
       God, I feel your power growing within.
       You fill me up, make strong my part to
       play in the blueprint of Your purpose.

I, your willing servant, ask
you to add unto me Lord, the courage
and strength I need to stand
strong, immovable among those
who stand on the front lines of
your battle for justice and for Truth.

I believe in me, I have Faith in You.

He Shall Give To You

Everything becomes new again;
spring has opened her bosom to release
the beautiful lilac and lavender
scent of her earthly perfume.
The sun arises bright and warm
in the eastern sky.

> I look into the sunrise of colour
> and dreams; surrealistic it seems,
> this view of heaven upon a western shore.
> As we emerge from winter's cocoon
> of frost and icy snow, spirit knows that
> warmth abounds in the spring of one's heart;
> we learn to impart, to share
> of the wealth He has placed on the
> inside of each temple which
> journeys this mortal world.

As spirit unfolds its wings
and learns to sing in this earthly place;
Grace enfolds you in God's
beautiful and merciful Love;
you will know peace.
For His beautiful white dove shall
alight upon your shoulder; guide you on
this path for all the days you shall live;
He shall give you this gift.

Salvation

Immaculate conception to
earthly rejection.
Benediction; crucifixion.
Blood flows, His Love shows;
forgiveness, deliverance.
Redemption.
Absolution, ascension .
Salvation, elation of
mortal soul, the spirit bright;
Child of God; sweet child of light.

I Walk With Thee, Lord

Lord, I hold onto thee as I watch
the rays of spring's magnificent
sun filter through the air
with the luminescent shimmer
of the wings of angels which surround us.
Rebirth: beginning ~ dream.
As evil tears apart the fabric of society's seams,
light holds back the darkness
as it tries to be free.

I walk with thee Lord, I walk with thee.

Lord, for every mistake I have made;
for every time I have not
considered another, you have found
forgiveness for me in your heart.
It is here I begin to follow your guidance
along the path of righteousness,
this place to which you lead.

I walk with thee Lord, I walk with thee.

Lord, for every hurt I have shown another,
for every child and every mother
may there be forgiveness, bounty, and peace
along the path to your promised land.
Though your path be narrow,
your kingdom hidden among
the stars, your gate is open wide
to the traveler with open arms,
the one who sees.

I walk with thee Lord, I walk with thee.

Stand Strong, Walk Tall

A searchlight from paradise
shines down upon the shores
of humanity.

> *Does He like what He sees?*

This ray of beautiful, brilliant
clear light, beaming
upon the tides of life's sea;
in you and in me there
is a beautiful story to tell.

> *I know Him so well within
> my heart, my world.*

His beam of light widens
and showers over the lands
close to my home.
There is a song to be sung;
there is music here and it
is ever clear what
it is I am to do.

> *Just take care of love; watch over peace;
> most important of all ~ stand strong, walk tall.*

Crescendo

His army rises.

> All nations, all colours,
> all creeds shall push back
> this evil darkness which
> now tries to overwhelm
> and destroy us.

> *Prophecy now slowly rises to a crescendo ...*
> *dust to dust.*

Leviathan Of Evil

Darkness has sent out his minions
among us to steal the souls of the
Father's children.

As I look at this leviathan of evil,
torment and fear, I have no reason
to feel this way …

    … *Christ walks with me here.*

He Comes

In the profoundest sense of time,
the angst buried within each
one of us who lives means nothing
on the seemingly blank canvas
of darkness as evil plays out its role
in the deepest, darkest cracks
and crevices of today's society.

Sobriety becomes more and more rare.
Many walk God's earth unaware of
His prophecy unfolding; holding
onto something that doesn't exist.

*Earthly bliss ne'er to be found
without the sound of trumpets clear;
when the heavenly sound of angelic
instrument is heard, there will be only
one word ~ the living Word.*

Christ.

A Special Gift

As I sit alone, pondering this Christmas,
I come to realize God's angels are all
around us; our celestial, loving guides.

      Without their gentle nudges
      what would become of me?
      So I open my heart and I feel their wings;
      hear their voices inside ~ I can see!

         This Christmas God's angels surrounded
         me with soft touches of energy;
         in the temple of my heart there is music:
         celestial, loving and free.

Warriors Of Truth

Sometimes, I feel like a tiger
trapped within the barred
and mortal bonds of humanity,
ever testing the boundaries placed
around my being by the
wiles of society's pretense and hypocrisy.
Challenging every seam,
every weakness, taking each
opportunity afforded to break free
of the conservitudes of leashed will.
Yet still, I have Faith in
the shining star of humankind.
Still, I walk forward, following the star
of my dreams, certain
that what seems illusion will
show itself to be my own special
part of the reality of inner peace.
At ease with the world around me,
ever humble in my view of my
fellow man, and this life so delicate;
so precious in the eyes of God.
His vast choir of angelic beings
share their radiant light, given freely
from His stores to replenish
the tired hearts of His faithful
and loving children;
His warriors of Truth
shine in me and in you.

[14]Chains of the Euphrates

Bound within the once mighty
Euphrates River, are the darkened
souls and fallen angels of eternity.

Prophecy unfolds, and this once
voluminous river is now down to,
in comparison, a trickle of its former
self.

*Woe be unto humanity when
the Euphrates dries and is no more;
two hundred thousand thousand
(200 million strong), souls of darkness
shall be released from their bondage,
upon mankind; at their hand, one
third of humanity shall perish.*

For you see, the Father is not
just love and mercy, he is also
wrath and judgment; make your
peace so you may rest eternally
within His Grace.

We know in our hearts His judgment is
just.

---

[14] *Dams on the Euphrates are now a threat as the water is down to a
mere trickle; almost completely dry. Prophecy continues to unfold.
Recently they discovered stairs leading to a dark, water filled cavern
under the Euphrates. It is now empty. Two hundred thousand
thousand (two hundred million), dark souls and fallen angels are now
loose within the world. At their hand, one third of humankind shall
perish.*

An Empty Page

If I sit and look at an empty page
for any extended, great length of time,
sooner or later a poem will appear
complete within its own rhyme.

> My eyes can see the words I need;
> heart paints pictures upon the page.
> In the place of creation's void
> the formative mind is engaged.

A hand that sits in a higher realm
pours freedom from the purest stream;
within the world engaged in rhyme
is the substance of the poet's dream.

> A word, an event, a song or a sight
> could trigger the most imaginative story;
> all of it comes from heaven's great place.
> Hallelujah! God's Love in its glory

Be Still

Such a glorious day
the Lord has blessed us with.
Hallelujah!

      Sun rises in the Eastern
      sky as the morning mist lies,
      unmoving, across the country
      fields.

Surely this is how we were
meant to live; alive in the warm
glow of His eternal Son-shine ~
light of the world and the spirit.

      I hear His quiet comfort in my
      heart; the Lord whispers, "Be
      still, for I Am come."

Temperance

I see stretched out before me
a river of dreams flowing
from my heart, becoming one
with universal soul.

      I am whole.

In the light of spirit
I have found myself.
I am learning to open wide
to my dreams, whatever
they may be: to experience,
to feel, to listen, to see peace
as a warm spring breeze
has found its way into,
and now surrounds, this world
of Love in which I live.
A world in which I give of this
mercy within me; share my
joy with plenteousness,
willing to give when a less
fortunate soul asks.
Learning to know kindness
in very simple tasks done
for and unto others.
I am being tempered and taught
      in patience: tolerance, gentleness
      of the human heart;
      in this state of parallel
      worlds, wisdom pearls in pools
      of stunning view ~ luminescent
      as the wings of angels,
      radiate through the outer

energies of my being.
Is this light I am seeing
of divine source?

> *Yes, of course ... and I choose*
> *to live this life within its glow.*

Shadow Dispelled

I watch the people on the street
      passing by, with their pretense
      and self-chosen separateness .
      How is it that they know not where
      or to what they are rushing;
      when spirit is met with immovable will
      and the choice of *not knowing* is made?
In this unknowing place events befall;
innocence has been corrupted ~
evil feasts and destroys from the inside out.
In this place of dreams there are so many kinds;
both good and bad.

      Conscious choice in the light dispels shadow of
        lingering iniquity wasting away in untruth
                  and contempt.

Lift up your eyes, let the vastness of beautiful
blue skies above you lift you up in your knowledge
and power of self.

      The "I Am" of mortal man; to judge no one,
      seek not vengeance nor redress.
      Time and God will give unto each according
      to their share.

Give Love, feel Love, lift Love up into
the heaven of your heart.
Forgive Love, receive Love, believe in Love.
Take time to know her and listen
to the wisdom of her lore.
Peace drifts in and out upon the tide
of this sea; it ebbs upon Love's shore.

Bridge To Freedom

A beam straight up to heaven shines
    a light which slices through dark skies.
    A backdrop of brilliance on the
    distant horizon and the bridge
    to freedom stands strong between.
    A dream, a hope, reflected upon
    the canvas of night's velvet;
    a view unlike any other to the
    eye of one's soul, a reminder of home
    seen through the jaded and feint
    glasses of mortal mind.
    One of a kind are we all,
    each, an individual expression
    of His Love and His hope
    for those righteous of heart.
    In peace, you impart wisdom
    to one who seeks, and help
    with answers for those who seek
    your wondrous works; miracles
    they have seen; like a dream.
    In between the sorrow
    and the joy, a new home
    is found which will astound
    the senses of spirit delight.

There will be no more sorrow,
there will exist no more night;
all is silent ~ all will be right.

Lines On My Face

Each line on my face tells a story
etched there by Grandfather time.
Complete with its sorrow, its tears and its joy;
each line, a story ~ lasting impressions
from this ever-changing world around me.
To what do I owe this portrait of
human weakness and strength merged
into one destiny, one hope, one heart?
To the tears that have formed their pathways
along the ridges of my skin, cleansing the
hurt and heartache which has shaded my soul;
to the pain; it has carved its healing upon
my essence; a dry river bed running
through the desert of my longing.
> Time casts shadows around me; they never
> truly leave but wait in the darkness, hoping
> that perhaps, with the right temptations,
> I will change my mind.
> So, I walk on through this world
> knowing that my heart belongs to the Father.
> I care not about this seduction which
> surrounds me, and I give less to the darkness
> from whence it has come.

> *I am a spirit of light and Truth;*
> *Created in His image, and placed upon the earth*
> *to shine as a beacon for those who have lost their way.*

Supersedence

Through the eyes of the tiger,
through the wild of the bear;
the feel and the heartbeat,
the fowl of the air.

    Aloft in His universe,
    wild in His forests, leaving
    the imprint of their passing upon
    the trails of earth's time and place.

        With the Grace and the ease of
        His life in the seas; we feign
        simplicity of this feat and
        take for granted the keep
        of His breath of Love;
        His touch of Faith in our free will.

Yet, we continue along this
path we walk, to wallow
in shadow still, its promise
hollow ~ no spirit to follow
the light of guidance as it leads.

    Materialistic requirements
    supersede spiritual needs.

Marionette

So many people rushing madly, doing so many things,
if you watch them closely run their road you may
notice puppet strings.
Like a marionette dancing upon an evening stage,
participating in the game of life so many like to play.
Minds have closed and hearts become stone
as they follow someone else's tune;
wonder how they got here when they see
only darkness in their room.
Broken hearts and promises lie hidden
behind every door; laughter is a thing of the past,
most don't know how to anymore.
Tears make up an ocean in the hearts
of those so blind; heartache follows constantly,
and never is it kind.

No one seems to care about
life's little riches anymore,
and peace is some elusive drea
found on some else's shore.
Madness creeps in slowly,
like too much baggage, all a game;
drowns the weakest souls in darkness,
those without a name.

Grey skies seem to hide the sun,
for those who cannot smile,
it's just too hard to walk this road,
cannot make another mile.
It is here, most fall down upon
their knees in humble prayer

You will see Love shining upon
God's sweet and golden, clear air.
Every night He watches over you
as you sleep and sends angels
who bring His answers to your prayers.

Fortress Of the Holy

I am being led on His path
of learning; shadow fades from
my view as the light brightens
around me.

      As I traverse this valley of
      the shadow of death I will fear not,
      for I have donned the armour
      of the Lord.

I have stored my riches
in the fortress of the Holy.

I have lit the candle of God within;
I kneel …

        … humility, prayer, Faith:
            believe, repent, evolve.

      All will be resolved upon this earth.
      There *shall be* renewal and peace.

        You will find comfort and rest
          in the fortress of the Holy.

Hand In Hand

Let me ever blossom in the light of the Creator's hand;
let me spread His beautiful words
to brothers and sisters in other lands.

> That I may bring the beauty of a
> glorious spring day
> to a child who sits in the war zone to play.

I will show the vibrant colour
of flowers to those bereft of sight,
and assist them in their view of life
tempering darkness with spiritual light.

> Pray let the scores of soldiers
> find their safe return to the shores of home;
> too young to be on such distant plains,
> far too young to feel so alone.

So come, rise up on your chariots strong,
sweep through mortal world and repair
what's gone wrong.
Shine your light through the darkness
of this glorious land.

> *Brothers and sisters,*
> *stand strong in your Faith hand to hand.*

Carried Upon the Ether

I heard the crying, weeping
and gnashing of teeth outside
the new kingdom ~ it is carried
upon the ether around
the world.

        Empaths cannot escape
        the sound of society's anguish
        and suffering.

Like an echo reverberating
again and again off the walls
of insanity.

Because of your vanity
you walk alone, struggling
through each day, relieved
when the hours pass and place
you in the deep darkness
of sleep.

A short reprieve before
the struggle begins again.

        Through the shallow view of your
        lenses it is impossible for you
        to see the deepest truths
        of reality.

So you plod along; no song
to help ease this darkness you
insist upon carrying.

Ahead of you coming into view;
a candle …

… you hope the light has
found you; getting brighter
all around you as you
sweep the dread of darkness
out your door.

Blessèd Be

Upon His head there'll be a crown;
silver chariot, stallions bound,
flaming wheels and thunderous
silence shall surround the wings
upon which he arrives.

> In His silence, He will look upon
> His Father's creation; His Father's children.
> We are all brothers and sisters;
> young siblings in Christ.

"Come up hither, my children.
To you, I shall give the glory of
my Father's kingdom.
To you, I will give the peace
of walking side by side
with the lion and the lamb.
To you, my blessèd children,
I will give the promise of eternity
and forgiveness, mercy; the truest
and purest of Love.
> You must learn to live in Truth;
> listen to Sister Wisdom, and allow
> Faith to be the ship in which
> you travel.

> For you shall be my witnesses
> to judgment and justice.
> You shall be the salt of creation
> to whom God's Eden shall be
> restored and returned.

Blessèd is he who believes in my Truth."

Amen

We shall pray.
Let us pray.
Amen.

Crystals in the air,
branches; all of nature
covered in lace.

Trees stand sentient
and still; stately witnesses
to mankind's great calamity.

As we, they too, weep
for humanity.

We shall pray.
Let us pray.
Amen.

May we never let go
our love of the sacred
and divine.

May we learn, once again,
to incorporate spirit return
to the Creator's great light
and care …

His hope is in the air;
all that is beautiful and just
will survive the storm.

We shall pray.
Let us pray.
Amen.

In Remembrance of Humanity: A Warning!

This work was channeled years before the creation of this book was ever considered. I am in awe of its content, and understand the truth contained within it. In order to create a new and beautiful world, (the way it was always meant to be), the old must be destroyed … destruction before renewal.

*Humanity has not **yet** become extinct; only by the Grace of the Father and His Holy and Sacred trinity, can humanity hope to survive. Hold no fear, for it is a tool of darkness.*

Faith, it is all about Faith.

There was a time when mortals walked Planet Earth. They were known as humankind; homo-sapiens. An increasingly arrogant lot, the more knowledge they gained, the more they feigned ignorance. Many generations ago it began. A handful of dark and very greedy, cold-hearted mortals, who possessed the wealth of Midas, realized in the early years, that most humans were easily fooled; self-absorbed, and blind to the illusion of reality that had begun building around them. They put into place a very dark plan, to lull as many as possible into a place of apathy; effectively mass hypnotizing society. As these dark mortals evolved, became smarter, wealthier; beginning to believe in their disillusioned sense of God-like status, their plans became darker: their tools stronger, their hearts colder and deeper in greed, their money bought whomever and whatever they needed to forward their illusion and create methods of making even more money, on the backs of a once strong society.

In the early days of planet earth and mortal occupancy, people thought in much simpler terms than they did just prior to their sudden extinction. People were not complex; they were indeed kind, and most worked together as a team to achieve what their societies required. Life was hard, but living was simple.

Society reached such an apathetic level they no longer questioned what their governments were doing. *They were taking care of the people.* That is where their troubles began; the train started coming off the track. The beauty of what life was created to be was hijacked and now, everything we hold dear, is being held for ransom by the dark and greedy side of the elitist's agenda.

As their science and knowledge increased; so too did their

ability to make bigger and better machines: apply new and improved medical techniques, and a multitude of toys which they purposely created to further separate humanity from one another. In order for humanity to function properly, it must function as a whole; for each was a part of the other, and so few realized it. Millions refused to awaken. World population had exploded to more than 20 billion. Genetic modification of food and of humans by evil capitalists, added to the cruel suffering created in many.

Was it not enough, mortals having had to deal with the natural toxins around them, that the man made ones which were crammed down their throats, added to the final death toll?

The society of man had become darker and darker in the end days. Machines became stronger, bigger *(in some cases much smaller),* and man had learned by then to incorporate free-thinking, artificial intelligence within them. Their arrogance and their mistaken sense that they were God-like, was their doom. Soon, all too soon, they would blink out of existence by the consequences of one foolish action.

When mankind began this mortal journey, the earth was a virtual garden of Eden; pristine and alive! By the 21st century, many had strayed from the true methods of recycling and ecology; taking care of the planet. They replaced their glass with plastic containers; pots and pans crafted from toxic metals, coated with toxic substances. They replaced safe packaging with all manner of plastic and other packaged, non-recyclable materials; effectively, becoming a *disposable* society. Society soon found themselves smothering in their own garbage and filth;

disease ran rampant.

Many illnesses were caused by new toxins; new pharmaceuticals *(generic);* generic then became the name of the game. Cheaper to mass produce, no healing involved; new problems caused. *More profit, more profit, more profit!*

No, it was no longer a world where people could be happy. It was no longer one of caring and kindness; but instead, became one of unbridled greed and madness.

The collective consciousness became toxic; the four tribes were not able to heal it as they had in past times. A few dark hearts within humankind took the many to the brink. So many good and kind warriors, struggled to fix what was broken, to raise the vibration of humanity; but it was broken beyond repair; they were not strong enough. The darkness had come to outweigh the light. Too many had let it continue much too long, and the tipping point had become an uncomfortable reality.

One would ask, *"Why did society, as a collective whole, not learn from their past mistakes."* I must admit, it also puts the writer of this work in a quandary trying to figure out the *"why?"*

Forests were destroyed, thousands upon thousands of acres at a time. The lungs of Mother earth found it increasingly difficult to survive. Tropical and temperate rainforests, being bull-dozed each day. Giant, ancient sentients being hewn with no concern for the health of the planet, nor anything or anyone that lives upon it; animals are dying in record numbers; entire species become extinct daily only to feed and puff up the ego of the trophy hunter;

to top up the greedy piles of money hoarded from the less fortunate.

Mankind had become the most vicious and dangerous predator on the planet. A bloodlust developed over centuries of war and abuse, that in the end, could never be satiated. *"I am entitled to more, more, more,"* as their combined, angry voices of lust, greed and violence became deafening to the masses. Not only were the people of the earth being held captive by the darkness; but were also controlled by fear. Tears and suffering were ignored. The satisfaction of the few was a priority; at *any* expense. To them, life was cheap, the good things could be bought, and if not bought; stolen.

I wish I had not been chosen to bring you this sad story of the disappearance of mankind. But alas, there must be a mortal messenger ~ anything else or anyone else, would not be understood. I will continue then, with the telling of the tale.

Mothers and fathers were given the task of caring for the little children; of protecting them and keeping them from harm. Instead, many were abused, abandoned, neglected or, frighteningly; worse. They were to care for the land, to watch over the health of this beautiful, living orb, and look at what was done to it. Each mortal was to blame. Some more than others; by allowing fear, control and *man* to guide them, they were all guilty of contributing to their destruction. Doing nothing, living apathetic and numb lives, gave the darkness free reign. More and more of the fearful were pulled into their webs of lies and deceit. They preyed on the weaker among them; easy, peasy ~ *no one was paying attention. They were all distracted by their toys: games and gladiator shows on television, and in sports arenas. Or worse, caught up in believing their illusions were the gospel of Truth.*

They continued struggling their way through the darkness and chaos; many had unwittingly allowed themselves to be surrounded. Some got lost in the darkness; others held captive in inhumane conditions. Then, there were the others; those who chose the dark and assisted fervently in creating yet more. Times were bleak; and quickly becoming even bleaker.

Self-centred and increasingly more insatiable, so many travelled the journey deaf and blind; the proverbial *head in the sand.*

In their last days, many parents became afraid of their children. They'd had their hands tied by society in utilizing effective methods of discipline. I will not discuss the heinous and unthinkable acts perpetrated upon children. This is not the place.

Empaths had the most difficult time in the societies of man toward the end days. The darker society became, the more the empath suffered, on increasingly deeper levels of soul. Darkness had become the norm. It covered everyone and everything; permeating the souls of weaker mortals. Suffering intensified: food and water was now poisoned, nutrition leached from the earth by their pesticides and man-made chemicals. Food was also poison; rotten to the core. With the genetic modification of food, it was no longer able to properly sustain the human's daily, healthy sustenance requirements. The air had become toxic; industries spewing chemicals and many other toxins into their atmosphere. With most forests now depleted, respiratory problems were running rampant.

From our societal position in the cosmos, we cannot imagine why mankind made the choices he did through those days. It was certain death for the entire species of humanoids. Sadly, they continued to live the future of their past. We were once a part of their past; now, we are broken hearted; the beauty, truly, was not meant to end, ever.

We shall continue the telling; though it hurts us deeply.

The Industrial revolution ~ was destroying the world. Multiple different industries started to churn out a variety of deadly toxins. I guess it was rationalized by telling themselves it was being sent skyward, it would just dissipate and disappear. No one paid attention to the cumulative effects and maladies it would bring about in future years. I shudder whenever I think of the shallow and narcissistic view that humans carried throughout those years. Those who did care were tired; exhausted from the struggle against these forces for generations. Too many were unwilling to give up their apathetic love for *things.* Their *"creature comforts";* Lord forbid they should lose any of their toys!

This was definitely *NOT* progress! It was regress. When mankind reached a certain point, he seemed to always prefer to go back to the past. Too many lived in the past; this was the *biggest, most destructive* energy of all. Too many vacated the now to return to their past. They were no longer emotionally available, not only to themselves, but to their children: their families, or the world. In the early 21st century, many, many good people tried to reverse this deadly path humanity was on. These good people spent endless hours and energy on bringing the

Truth of Reality to the masses. Each time they tried, it left them with a little more sadness, they became more disillusioned with circumstance. Regardless, they continued the spiritual struggle, they knew there was much to hope for. Unfortunately, their numbers grew far too slowly. It was taking years, upon years, for others to wake up. Many did so, reluctantly, but they did. Many just, one day, looked around and felt the inspiration to help in areas that were the weakest; to man up the forces fighting for the salvation of the beautiful planet. They have been, and will continue to be, rewarded at the time of their evolution to the next Spiritual level. Evolution was at hand; many would not survive the physical, emotional and psychological alterations that would be necessary to make that evolutionary step. But, that was truly okay ... all would be well upon their return home.

Finally, the political situation on Planet Earth truly became idiotic. Mortals are much, much more intelligent than they behaved. They had the wisdom of internal guidance, spiritual assistance; so very few of you availed yourselves of that information; or, did not believe it when you did. So few among humanity, had the strength and grit to stand against the masses, for, in those years, the powerful usually got rid of them in very stealthful and ingenious ways. They were good at performing acts of smoke and mirrors; creating the numerous illusions that would hogwash the eyes of mankind. Never were there so many malicious human spirits gathered together in one place at a time as at political functions. They were all so eager to steal from society. Holding knives at one another's back, whilst at the same time, smiling in their hypocrisy of the friendship they *profess to offer*.

We placed a message within one of the crop circles which

we placed on your earth many years ago, in ASCII system language. We knew you would understand and be able to read it:

"Beware the bearers of FALSE gifts and their BROKEN PROMISES. Much PAIN but still time. BELIEVE. There is GOOD out there. We OPPOSE DECEPTION. Conduit CLOSING (BELL SOUND)."

How much simpler did we need to put it ~ but still, you did not understand; or, I should say, understood, but refused to pay it any heed. There were many among you who listened. Unless all were united, it mattered not the good wisdom you held close. To make such a grand step in the evolutionary ladder, mankind needed to be unified as a whole; that clearly, would never happen.

Your bible, though translated over the centuries by *man*, still held true. Society needed to learn to live in Grace, with compassion for one another. Much may have been learned by reading this good book. I am not talking about reading in a *religious* sense; but rather, reading it in a *spiritual* sense. Too many took this book in a *literal* capacity. It was a book of parables; riddles, in a sense. Those who were *truly* spiritual, would understand how to *read between the lines*. In the end, these were the things and attitudes which destroyed mortal society and wiped out humankind:

The love of money and materialistic lifestyles
The Industrial Revolution
The Technological Age
Industry
Capitalism
Greed
Hate
Racism
Hypocrisy
Ego
Mental Illness, much of it caused by stresssors and the
pharmacological bandaids offered to ease it.
Drugs
Rape
Incest
Torture
Abuse of animals, children and each other
Nuclear power and mass weapons of war
Man's Inhumanity to Man

This list could go on and on and on. You fed the darkness
and starved the light.

I mentioned earlier that I had lived on the earth in mortal
form during the early part of the 21st century. I Am a
Human spirit who evolved in those years. We know only
bliss here ~ our mortal ways; long forgotten. We do
lament the extinction of mortals. We welcome those souls
of the light who now continue in their evolutionary career.
When light souls leave earth, leaving the ashes of their
mortal vessel behind, they are immediately taken to a
place of great healing by our transport angels. All
hardships: pain, suffering, sorrow, darkness ~ disappear.
They cannot follow. None of the light souls received are
ever broken beyond repair, for we have the means to heal

mortal damage to the indwelling soul. That being said, there are the few who make the choice not to continue. Our hearts break each time a piece of our whole makes this choice. They are immediately re-merged with the light energy of creation; they no longer have any type of consciousness, with the exception of that of the whole. Each time one of the Creator's souls makes this choice; a tear falls from the world of bliss. That is among the many reasons for rain on earth. As you can imagine; or perhaps, not, each tear that falls from the Creator's eye, replenishes and heals that which dwells upon Planet Earth.

I know, during my time as a mortal, I too fell into all the same traps and illusions. I do not regret (for that is a human emotion, not known here), but am aware of my own mortal contributions to the calamity. I sinned, I threw out garbage, *(prior to the recycle movement),* and occasionally reveled in the darkness.

The scenario I have described herein could be real. As our message stated:

"There is still time. BELIEVE," still holds true. But, it must be done soon, very soon. This is a warning to the people of Planet Earth. Turn it around now. We have no wish to mourn your extinction. You are one of the Creator's greatest works of Art. You are, each and every one of you, a masterpiece!"

The mortal messenger that has delivered this insight, was chosen due to the clarity of the channel. Ah, what a better one to choose, a *poet*; one who forever dreams of a better world.

Keep the Arts ALIVE. Keep on with your PRAYER. Hold onto your FAITH in the FATHER. Continue your KINDNESS and COMPASSION. Strive for UNITY, ONENESS even in the face of adversity, and you might, you just might, be able to heal the damage that has been done, and change the course of Spaceship Earth. Only then can this Planet be settled in the blissful and loving ways of Light and Life.

Biography
Deborah L. Kelly

Deborah L. Kelly is a transplanted Easterner who found this beautiful province of British Columbia at seventeen years old, and decided this was *the* place to be … all the hippies were here!

In 2010, after a corporate career of many years, *Deborah* began a new way of living; she had found the magic and wonder of the world of poetry.
Working closely with Candice James, *New Westminster Poet Emerita,,* and Janet Kvammen, President of *Royal City Literary Arts Society, Deborah* was elected to the Board. After two years with *RCLAS, Ms. Kelly* published her first book *Through My Eyes* in 2015 with Silver Bow Publishing.

Comes the Storm is a book *Ms. Kelly* has been called to write. This will be *Deborah's* seventh published book of poetry. In a world gone so terribly wrong we need to encourage and inspire others.

Deborah L. Kelly is an award winning poet and short story writer. Published both internationally and nationally in a myriad of various anthologies and newsletters, she continues to write poetry throughout her retirement. She lives the country life in Northern BC and loves every minute of it: writing, gardening and living the amazing blessings of watching her grandchildren grow up. *Deborah* may be reached at <u>poetrybydeborah@gmail.com</u>. [15]"Lifting these words unto Heaven, all glory is given unto the Divine; without the Trinity of the blessèd *Father, Son and Holy Spirit*, we have nothing."

Other books by Deborah L. Kelly:

Through My Eyes
Spirit'Song
Heartworks
Cry of Humanity
Songs of the North
Glass Houses
Upon the Page (Chapbook)

---

[15] *The Spiritual meaning of the Angelic number 111 (the number of pages in this book), as described by Chris Jones of The Habitat (thehabitat.com):*

"The number 111 contains two significant numbers in numerology: one and eleven. The number one represents independence and motivation. It also signifies new beginnings and the ability to let go and move forward towards success. Eleven is powerful and indicates your ongoing or impending discovery of your soul's mission and life purpose. Combined, the numbers are doubly significant, harkening spiritual awakening and inspiration."